I Learn to Tell the Truth

Carolyn Nystrom

Illustrated by
Dwight Walles

MOODY PRESS
CHICAGO

© 1990 BY
CAROLYN NYSTROM

All rights reserved. No part of this book may be reproduced in any form without permission in writing from the publisher, except in the case of brief quotations embodied in critical articles or reviews.

Moody Press, a ministry of the Moody Bible Institute, is designed for education, evangelization, and edification. If we may assist you in knowing more about Christ and the Christian life, please write us without obligation: Moody Press, c/o MLM, Chicago, IL 60610

ISBN : 0-8024-6175-1

Printed in the United States of America

1 2 3 4 5 6 7 8 Printing/DP/Year 94 93 92 91 90

"It was the biggest fish in the whole lake!" My arms stretched wide from end to end. "That fish pulled my line out as far as it would go. My dad had to help." My voice got higher and higher. "We worked the line. Even my dad got tired. Finally we hoisted the fish into the boat."

I could see my friend Brad's eyes get bigger and bigger. I had wanted Brad to go with us on the fishing trip, but he had to play soccer instead. So I was showing him how much he'd missed. "That fish flopped around the bottom of the boat so hard, we thought he'd tip us over."

"What happened then?" I could hear the gasp in Brad's voice.

"Oh, he wore out," I said. "Then Mom cooked him for dinner."

Colossians 3:9; James 3:5-6

It was a great story—the best of the season. Only none of it was true. Not much of it anyway. Well, our family *had* gone fishing. And I *had* seen a big fish—in the lake. But that smart fish never got near my hook.

Then why did I tell Brad such a lie? I'm not sure.

Maybe I was just angry that Brad had not come with us on the trip. Maybe I just wanted to brag a little that I was big and tough and could handle a huge fish.

    Brad was impressed all right. He told all of our friends about my big fish. I thought I would feel proud, but I didn't. I just felt guilty inside. And that fish story started a lot of trouble. Not for Brad. For me.

A few days later, Mom was making a fancy dinner for my grandma's birthday. Mom planned all of Grandma's favorite foods: roast beef and corn and tossed salad and mashed potatoes and gravy and cherry pie. I'm glad Grandma likes cherry pie, because I like it too.

"Jeremy," Mom said as she peeked into the living room. "You've got to pick up your toys. You know your grandma has trouble seeing. I don't want her to trip and fall."

"I will, Mom," I promised. "I'll put them away fast just as soon as I see her coming."

Matthew 5:33-37

But when I looked out the window and saw Grandma, I was in the middle of building a big bridge. All of my toy cars were lined up to go over it as soon as I had it finished. Boats were lined up to go underneath. "Sure, I promised," I said to myself, "but maybe Mom will forget."

A moment later, Grandma was in the living room reaching to give me a big hug. Even though her eyes were on me, I could see her feet heading straight for my bridge. Mom saw it too — and caught Grandma just in time. But not in time to save my bridge. Pieces flew in all directions.

"Jeremy, you promised," Mom said.

I didn't like the disappointed look in Mom's eyes, so I turned away.

Lie trouble at school was next. My teacher wanted me to write my spelling words five times. I started to write the words at school, but I didn't finish. So I took them home. I meant to do the work, but I forgot.

Next morning, Mrs. Day said, "Jeremy, where is your spelling paper?"

I looked at the floor for a minute and tried to think what to do. If I told Mrs. Day the truth, I'd have to write spelling words during recess. Everyone else would go outdoors to play. I didn't want that to happen, so I lied.

Proverbs 12:19

"I wrote the words last night, Mrs. Day," I said. Mrs. Day looked doubtful, so I decided to make up a little story, so she'd be more likely to believe me.

"I wrote all the words five times, just like you said," I told her. "But my school bus came early this morning, and I had to run. So I left the paper on the counter right beside my milk. I'll be sure to bring it tomorrow." And I smiled as well as I could.

I hoped Mrs. Day wouldn't call my mom to check my story. But I couldn't help noticing that lying was getting easier all the time. *Maybe if she does call, I can lie to Mom too,* I thought.

After school, Brad and I got off the school bus together. My mom sometimes gives us both a snack before Brad goes on to his own house. So we ran up to my porch together. Brad leaped over the steps and landed with a thud on the porch. I leaped over the steps and landed with a sprawling squash in my mom's new flower bed. I picked myself up, brushed at the mud on my pants, and headed for the door.

Exodus 20:16; Proverbs 19:5

Just then, Mom came out. She took one look at her smashed flowers and said, "Who—?"

But I cut her off. Before I even thought about it, a lie came out. "Brad did it," I yelled.

I tried not to look at Brad, but I could see surprise and hurt in his eyes. I could also see my fish story evaporate from his mind.

Mom wasn't convinced either. Maybe it was the mud on my pants. Maybe Mrs. Day really had called. Maybe Mom remembered my toys on the floor. Maybe she'd heard about my fish story. But Mom's voice got slow and quiet, just the way it always does when I know I'm in trouble.

"Brad, you'd better go home now," Mom said. "Jeremy and I have to talk."

It was a long hard talk at out kitchen table. Mom began by asking how I felt when I told a lie. I had to think about that for a little bit, because I felt different ways at different times. At first, telling a lie was hard, and I felt bad for a long time afterward. But later it got easier, and I almost enjoyed planning ways to get away with it. But I didn't plan that last lie about Brad falling into the flowers at all. It just came out of my mouth.

Romans 7:14-24; Hebrews 13:18

"That's the way lying is," Mom said. "It's called the lie trap. And it traps the person who is doing the lying."
 I didn't feel like I was in a trap, but maybe I was.

"God gave you a conscience," Mom went on. "That's the part of you that makes you want to do what is right."

I had to agree that telling the truth seemed better most of the time.

"But if you don't do what your conscience makes you feel is right," Mom went on, "it gets easier and easier to do wrong. You are in the lie trap."

I gulped.

Proverbs 12:22; Romans 6:12-14

"Lying traps you in another way too," Mom went on.

I didn't want to ask how.

"What were you going to tell me about your spelling paper, Jeremy?"

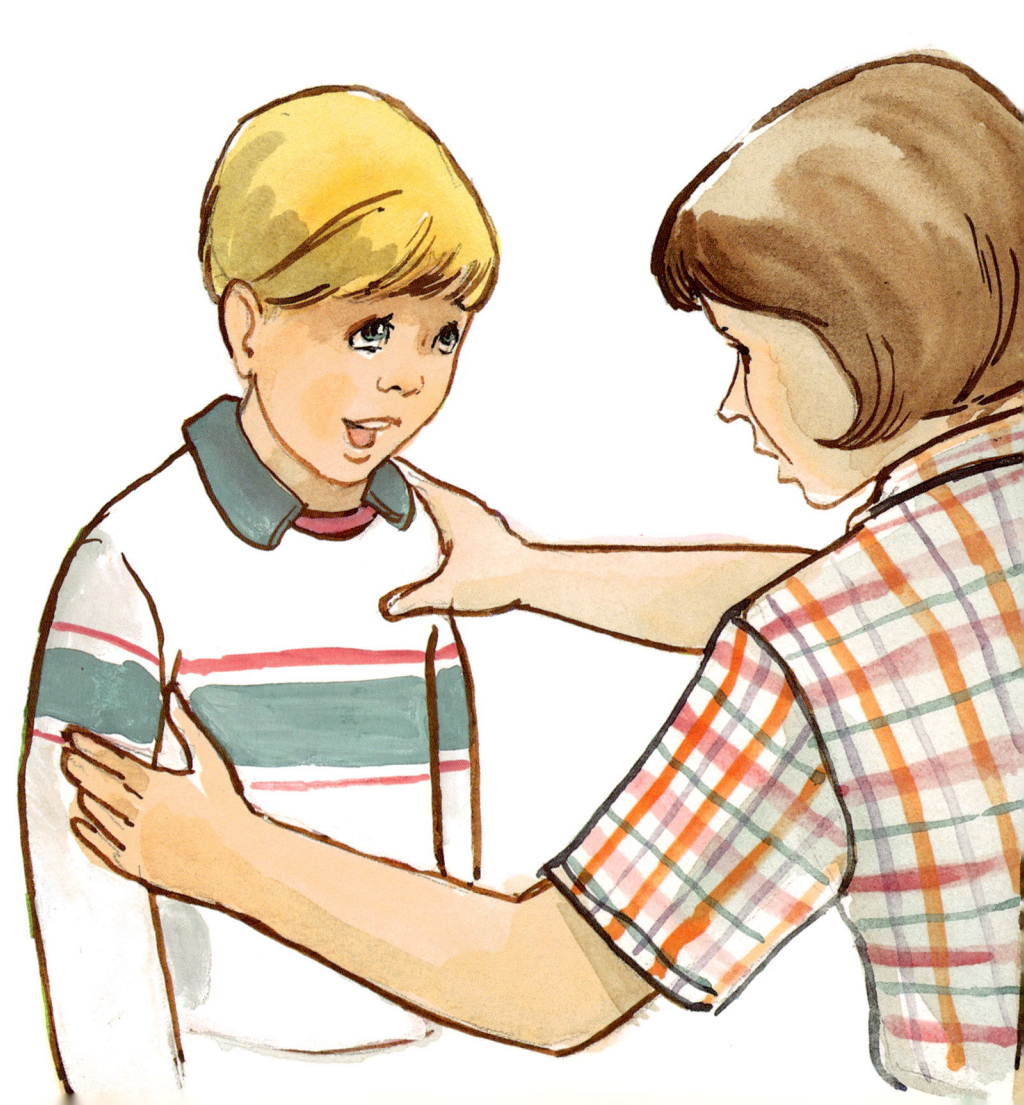

I looked at the floor. "I was going to say that I lost it."
"Did you?"
"No."
"Then why were you going to tell me that?"
"Because I already told Mrs. Day that I did the work."
"That's another lie trap, Jeremy," Mom said. "Sometimes a person has to keep on lying, just to cover up what he's already said."

James 3:9-10; Ephesians 5:8-9

It took a long time for people to trust me again. One time I really did forget to bring a school paper. But I could see that Mrs. Day didn't believe what I told her about it. When I told Mom, she looked straight at my eyes for a long time before she finally said, " All right, Jeremy." I guess Mom didn't believe my promises either. When I told her that I'd sweep the grass off the driveway, she kept coming out to see if I was really doing the work.

But the hardest part was Brad. Brad never did say anything more about my fish story. But he started telling some pretty tall tales of his own — stories about race cars and airplane trips. And once Brad blamed me for pushing a girl on the school playground. But I was never near her! I guess maybe lying is catching. And Brad caught it from me.

Psalm 51:6; Proverbs 3:3; Philippians 4:8

I'm glad I decided to get out of the lie trap. But it wasn't as easy as I had thought. Sometimes a lie came into my mind even before the truth did. So I had to tell myself to talk more slowly and to think first what I was going to say. And I had to remind myself that sometimes even telling the truth would get me into trouble.

Once Dad was in the middle of fixing our screen door. He yelled, "Who broke my skill saw?"

Just the day before, I had stepped on the saw by accident. So I took a deep breath, went over to my dad, and said, "I broke it, Dad. It was an accident. I'm sorry." I had to buy Dad a new saw with my own money. Telling a lie would have been easier. But I could see that Dad was glad that I had told him the truth.

Telling the truth, even when it got me into trouble, helped my parents to trust me again.

Titus 1:2; John 4:24; 1 Corinthians 13:6; Psalm 33:4

It was hard to stop lying, but I'm glad that I did. Lying is wrong. So I told God that I was sorry that I had been telling lies. And I asked Him to help me stop. I know that sometimes, when a lie was just ready to come out of my mouth, it was God who reminded me to tell the truth. And I stopped.

Once in a while, though, I don't stop in time. I lie. But then I remember what it was like to be in the lie trap. And I don't want to get into the lying habit again. So I ask God to forgive me. Then I tell the person I lied to the truth.

I know that God wants what is good for me. He will help me tell the truth because He loves me. He wants me to be like Him.
And God doesn't lie.